Imitation In Writing
AESOP'S FABLES

Background:

We are commanded in Scripture to imitate the Lord Jesus Christ. We are also commanded to imitate those brothers and sisters who through faith and patience have inherited the promises. To imitate something or someone means:

- To do or try to do after the manner of; to follow the example of; to copy in action.
- To make or produce a copy or representation of; to copy, reproduce.
- To be, become, or make oneself like; to assume the aspect or semblance of; to simulate.

    This God-sanctioned method of learning is an essential tool for educating young people. For example, how is it that we teach a child to perform simple physical skills such as throwing and catching? "Hold your hands **like this**. Step forward as you throw **like this**." – Imitation. How is it that we teach a child how to form his letters correctly? "Hold your pencil **like this**. Look at **this 'a'**. Trace **this letter**. Now, you try to make an 'a' **like this one**." – Imitation. How is it that we teach art? At Logos School students learn how to paint by imitating master painters of the past. "**This** is a good painting. Let's see if you can **reproduce it**." – Imitation. How is it that music is taught, or reading, or math? Very often the best instruction in any of these areas necessarily includes imitation. Why, when it comes to teaching young people writing do we educators regularly neglect this effective tool?

    Educators in seventeenth century England knew the value of imitation as a tool through which they could teach style, particularly in the area of writing. The primary method of imitation in these English grammar schools was called ***Double Translation***. In a double translation the teacher would translate a Latin work into English. The student was to copy this English translation over, paying close attention to every word and its significance. Then the student was to write down the English and Latin together, one above the other, making each language answer to the other. Afterwards the student translated the original Latin to English on his own. This was the first part of the translation. The second part took place ten days afterward when the student was given his final English translation and required to turn it back into good Latin.

    Benjamin Franklin wrote of a similar exercise that he employed to educate himself a century later. When he was a young man he came across a particular piece of writing that he delighted in, *The Spectator*. *The Spectator* is a series of 555 popular essays published in 1711 and 1712. These essays were intended to improve manners and morals, raise the cultural level of the middle-class reader, and popularize serious ideas in science and philosophy. They were written well, the style was excellent, and Franklin wanted to imitate it. Here is Franklin's method of "double translation" regarding *The Spectator:*

> With that view (imitating this great work) I took some of the papers, and making short hints of the sentiments in each sentence, laid them by a few days, and then, without looking at the book, tried to complete the papers again, by expressing each hinted sentiment at length, and as fully as it had been expressed before, in any suitable words that should occur to me. Then I compared my Spectator with the original, discovered some of my faults, and corrected them.

But he realized that he needed a greater stock of words in order to add variety and clarity of thought to his writing.

> Therefore I took some of the tales in the Spectator, and turned them into verse; and, after a time, when I had pretty well forgotten the prose, turned them back again. I also sometimes jumbled my collection of hints into confusion, and after some weeks endeavored to reduce them into the best order, before I began to form the sentences and complete the subject. This was to teach me method in the arrangement of thoughts. By comparing my work with the original, I discovered many faults and corrected them; but I sometimes had the pleasure to fancy that, in particulars of small consequence, I had been fortunate enough to improve the method or the language, and this encouraged me to think that I might in time become to be a tolerable English writer, of which I was extremely ambitious.

Now the question is; "How can we employ a similar methodology?"

Imitation In Writing
AESOP'S FABLES

Instructions:

1. CHOOSE A STUDENT-READER: Send the fable home with a student the night before you begin the assignment. He should be prepared to read the fable for the class the next day. If you begin the assignment on Monday the fable can be given to a student early in the day so that he has time to prepare a bit before reading for the class.

2. READ SILENTLY: Have the students read the fable quietly to themselves, paying close attention to the story line. When they are done, they should underline the vocabulary words in the fable. Discuss, by means of questioning, who the characters are in the fable and what took place.

3. STUDENT READS FABLE: The student who was selected earlier to read the fable now comes to the front of the class and reads it.

4. ORAL RETELLING: The teacher calls on individual students to retell the fable in their own words. These oral summaries should be short and to the point.

5. CHARACTERS: At this point the students will list the main characters in the story.

6. VOCABULARY: Call on one student for each of the vocabulary words. That student will read the sentence in which the word is found, providing context, and then define the word for the class. Occasionally the student definition will need to be modified by the teacher so that it is an exact match with the vocabulary word in the fable. One word definitions work well. The idea here is to provide the students with a synonym for each vocabulary word which could be substituted into the sentence without distorting the meaning. Have the students write the definition of each word on the blank provided.

7. OUTLINE THE PLOT: At this point the students will go through the fable and summarize the plot one sentence at a time. Each fable has been divided by superscript numbers which correspond to the numbered blanks below, showing how to organize the outline. If the sentence or phrase being outlined contains a vocabulary word, it must be included as one of the words in the outline. These vocabulary words must be underlined in the outline to identify them as such. Initially this activity should be guided by the teacher and completed as a class. Providing every-other simple sentence or phrase for each section is helpful for younger students. There is some room for variation in the exact wording of the sentence or phrase.

8. CLIP & PASS IN ORIGINAL FABLE: Before the students begin rewriting the fable they must cut along the dotted line and pass the original text in. Some students will want to read through the fable one more time to better understand the sequence of the story.

9. WRITE FIRST DRAFT: The students are now ready to rewrite the fable using their outline to guide them. I allow my students to change the characters and some of the incidentals of the story in their rewrites as long as the original plot is identifiable. The exceptionally good writers in the class will thrive off of this opportunity to be innovative. The students who are less comfortable with writing will tend to stick to the same characters and incidentals, that is fine. All of the vocabulary

words must be used correctly and underlined in the rewrite. The students should skip lines on the first draft to allow room for editing.

10. EDITING: Students take their rewrites home for the parents to edit. This is most profitable when the parents sit down with the student and edit the fable together. Guidelines for editing can be sent home at the beginning of the year or communicated at Back to School Night so that parents know what is expected. I require that the edited first draft be due Thursday if the assignment was given Monday. This gives parents and students a few days to complete and edit the fable.

11. FINAL DRAFT: Time in class is provided for the students to work on the final draft. The students should not skip lines. I allow the students to draw a rubric at the beginning of their story if they like.

12. ASSIGNMENT DUE: The final draft will be due on Friday. They should turn in three items stapled together in the following order: Final Draft, First Draft and Outline. From time to time it is beneficial for the students to read their rewrites for the class. This activity could be scheduled on Friday when they are due.

13. GRADING: The grading sheet should be duplicated, cut out, completed, and stapled to each student's rewrite. This will help the teacher to focus on the essential aspects of the composition as he is grading it and will provide specific feedback to the student and parents regarding which areas will need more attention in the future. As a rule, I deduct one point for each mistake per page for sentence structure, spelling, capitalization and punctuation.

Proposed Schedule: (grades 2 and up)

Monday	Steps 1-9 (see instructions above)	60 minutes
Tues. & Wed.	Step 10	(no class time)
Thursday	Step 11	30 minutes
Friday	Steps 12-13	(as desired)

Student Example:

The Fox and the Woodcutter

[1]A fox, running before the hounds, came across a woodcutter <u>felling</u> an oak and begged him to show him a safe hiding-place. [2]The woodcutter advised him to take shelter in his own hut, so the fox crept in and hid himself in a corner. [3]The huntsman soon came up with his hounds and <u>inquired</u> of the woodcutter if he had seen the fox. [4]He declared that he had not seen him, and yet pointed, all the time he was speaking, to the hut where the fox lay hidden. [5]The huntsman took no notice of the signs, but believing his word, hastened forward in the chase. [6]As soon as they were well away, the fox departed without taking any notice of the woodcutter. [7]Whereon he called to him and <u>reproached</u> him, saying, [8]"You ungrateful fellow, you owe your life to me, and yet you leave me without a word of thanks." [9]The fox replied, "Indeed, I should have thanked you fervently if your deeds had been as good as your words, and if your hands had not been <u>traitors</u> to your speech."

✂ ---

The Fox and the Woodcutter   Name: *Example*

I. List the characters in this fable: *fox, hounds, woodcutter, huntsman*

II. Vocabulary: <u>Underline</u> the vocabulary words in the fable, and define them below.

1. felling: *cutting down*   3. reproached: *scolded*
2. inquired: *asked*   4. traitors: *betrayers*

III. Outline this fable using a three or four word sentence or phrase for each numbered section. Be sure to include and <u>underline</u> all of the vocabulary words in this outline.

1. *Fox begs <u>felling</u> woodcutter.*   6. *Fox escapes without notice.*
2. *Woodcutter hides fox.*   7. *Woodcutter <u>reproaches</u> fox.*
3. *Huntsman with hounds <u>inquires</u>.*   8. *"I saved you!?!"*
4. *Woodcutter declares but points.*   9. *"Your hands are <u>traitors</u>."*
5. *Huntsman misses signs.*

IV. Cut along the dotted line to remove the original fable. Rewrite this fable using your outline. Include and <u>underline</u> the vocabulary words in your rewrite. Check your work for the following: neat and graceful handwriting, title, indentation, spelling, punctuation.

<u>Student Rewrite:</u>

The Fox and the Woodcutter
(by Laurel McGarry – 3rd Grade)

     A fox, who was being chased by hounds, came panting up to a woodcutter who was <u>felling</u> an oak and begged him to give him a safe place to hide. The woodcutter quickly advised the fox to take shelter under a piece of wood that he kept on the windowsill in his hut. Soon afterward the huntsman came and <u>inquired</u>, "Have you seen a fox? For I am chasing one." The woodcutter replied, "No, I have not seen hide nor hair of this fox you speak of (but all the time the woodcutter was pointing to his window where you could see a few red hairs of the fox). The huntsman took no notice of the signs but believed what he had heard and was off like a jackrabbit being chased by a dog. After the huntsman was quite gone the fox came out and started off in the opposite direction of the huntsman. The woodcutter <u>reproached</u> him and said, "You ungrateful, obstinate – thing!! You have no right to be called a fox!!" The fox's response was, "I would have thanked you fervently if your hand had not been a <u>traitor</u> to your speech, for I saw you point to me when you spoke to the huntsman." "You," screamed the woodcutter, "You – You'll pay for this!! I'm going to fell a tree on you!! I'll wipe out all the foxes in the world!! I'll do something really, really awful to you when you're not looking!!!!"

Finis

AESOP'S FABLES

Plot Outline	10	_____
Handwriting	10	_____
Vocab. Usage	20	_____
Sentence Structure	15	_____
Spell./Punct./ Cap.	25	_____
Story Line	20	_____
Total	100	_____

AESOP'S FABLES

Plot Outline	10	_____
Handwriting	10	_____
Vocab. Usage	20	_____
Sentence Structure	15	_____
Spell./Punct./ Cap.	25	_____
Story Line	20	_____
Total	100	_____

AESOP'S FABLES

Plot Outline	10	_____
Handwriting	10	_____
Vocab. Usage	20	_____
Sentence Structure	15	_____
Spell./Punct./ Cap.	25	_____
Story Line	20	_____
Total	100	_____

AESOP'S FABLES

Plot Outline	10	_____
Handwriting	10	_____
Vocab. Usage	20	_____
Sentence Structure	15	_____
Spell./Punct./ Cap.	25	_____
Story Line	20	_____
Total	100	_____

AESOP'S FABLES

Plot Outline	10	_____
Handwriting	10	_____
Vocab. Usage	20	_____
Sentence Structure	15	_____
Spell./Punct./ Cap.	25	_____
Story Line	20	_____
Total	100	_____

AESOP'S FABLES

Plot Outline	10	_____
Handwriting	10	_____
Vocab. Usage	20	_____
Sentence Structure	15	_____
Spell./Punct./ Cap.	25	_____
Story Line	20	_____
Total	100	_____

AESOP'S FABLES

Plot Outline	10	_____
Handwriting	10	_____
Vocab. Usage	20	_____
Sentence Structure	15	_____
Spell./Punct./ Cap.	25	_____
Story Line	20	_____
Total	100	_____

AESOP'S FABLES

Plot Outline	10	_____
Handwriting	10	_____
Vocab. Usage	20	_____
Sentence Structure	15	_____
Spell./Punct./ Cap.	25	_____
Story Line	20	_____
Total	100	_____

The Viper and the File

[1]A viper, entering the workshop of a smith, [2]sought from the tools the means of satisfying his hunger. [3]He more particularly addressed himself to a file, [4]and asked him the favor of a meal. [5]The file replied, [6]"You must indeed be a simple-minded fellow if you expect to get anything from me, [7]who am accustomed to take from everyone, [8]and never to give anything in return."

The Viper and the File   Name:_____

I. List the characters in this fable:_____

II. Vocabulary: <u>Underline</u> the vocabulary words in the fable, and define them below.

1. viper:_____   3. particularly:_____

2. means:_____   4. addressed:_____

III. Outline this fable using a three or four word sentence or phrase for each numbered section. Be sure to include and <u>underline</u> all of the vocabulary words in this outline.

1._____   5._____
2._____   6._____
3._____   7._____
4._____   8._____

IV. Cut along the dotted line to remove the original fable. Rewrite this fable using your outline. Include and <u>underline</u> the vocabulary words in your rewrite. Check your work for the following: neat and graceful handwriting, title, indentation, spelling, punctuation.

The Ants and the Grasshopper

¹The ants were spending a fine winter's day drying grain collected in the summertime. ²A grasshopper, perishing with famine, ³passed by and earnestly begged for a little food. ⁴The ants inquired of him, ⁵"Why did you not treasure up food during the summer?" ⁶He replied, "I had not leisure enough. ⁷I passed the days in singing." ⁸They then said in derision: "If you were foolish enough to sing all the summer, you must dance supperless to bed in the winter."

The Ants and the Grasshopper   Name:_____

I. List the characters in this fable:_____

II. Vocabulary: <u>Underline</u> the vocabulary words in the fable, and define them below.

1. perishing:_____   3. inquired:_____
2. earnestly:_____   4. leisure:_____

III. Outline this fable using a three or four word sentence or phrase for each numbered section. Be sure to include and <u>underline</u> all of the vocabulary words in this outline.

1._____   5._____
2._____   6._____
3._____   7._____
4._____   8._____

IV. Cut along the dotted line to remove the original fable. Rewrite this fable using your outline. Include and <u>underline</u> the vocabulary words in your rewrite. Check your work for the following: neat and graceful handwriting, title, indentation, spelling, punctuation.

The Crow and the Pitcher

¹A crow perishing with thirst saw a pitcher, ²and hoping to find water, flew to it with delight. ³When he reached it, he discovered to his grief that it contained so little water that he could not possibly get at it. ⁴He tried everything he could think of to reach the water, but all his efforts were in vain. ⁵At last he collected as many stones as he could carry and dropped them one by one with his beak into the pitcher, ⁶until he brought the water within his reach and thus saved his life.

⁷Necessity is the mother of invention.

The Crow and the Pitcher   Name:_____

I. List the characters in this fable:_____

II. Vocabulary: <u>Underline</u> the vocabulary words in the fable, and define them below.

1. perishing:_____ 3. vain:_____

2. grief:_____ 4. necessity:_____

III. Outline this fable using a three or four word sentence or phrase for each numbered section. Be sure to include and <u>underline</u> all of the vocabulary words in this outline.

1._____ 5._____

2._____ 6._____

3._____ 7._____

4._____

IV. Cut along the dotted line to remove the original fable. Rewrite this fable using your outline. Include and <u>underline</u> the vocabulary words in your rewrite. Check your work for the following: neat and graceful handwriting, title, indentation, spelling, punctuation.

The Fox and the Grapes

[1]A famished fox saw some clusters of ripe black grapes hanging from a trellised vine. [2]She resorted to all her tricks to get at them, [3]but wearied herself in vain, for she could not reach them. [4]At last she turned away, hiding her disappointment and saying: [5]"The grapes are sour, and not ripe as I thought."

[6]It is easy to despise what you know you cannot possess.

✂ --

The Fox and the Grapes   Name:_____

I. List the characters in this fable:_____

II. Vocabulary: <u>Underline</u> the vocabulary words in the fable, and define them below.

1. famished:_____   3. vain:_____
2. resorted:_____   4. despise:_____

III. Outline this fable using a three or four word sentence or phrase for each numbered section. Be sure to include and <u>underline</u> all of the vocabulary words in this outline.

1._____   4._____
2._____   5._____
3._____   6._____

IV. Cut along the dotted line to remove the original fable. Rewrite this fable using your outline. Include and <u>underline</u> the vocabulary words in your rewrite. Check your work for the following: neat and graceful handwriting, title, indentation, spelling, punctuation.

The Wolf and the Goat

[1]A wolf saw a goat feeding at the summit of a steep precipice, [2]where he had no chance of reaching her. [3]He called to her and earnestly begged her to come lower down, lest she fall by some mishap; [4]and he added that the meadows lay where he was standing, and that the herbage was most tender. [5]She replied, "No, my friend, it is not for the pasture that you invite me, [6]but for yourself, who are in want of food."

✂ --

The Wolf and the Goat   Name:_____

I. List the characters in this fable:_____

II. Vocabulary: <u>Underline</u> the vocabulary words in the fable, and define them below.

1. precipice:_____   3. mishap:_____

2. earnestly:_____   4. herbage:_____

III. Outline this fable using a three or four word sentence or phrase for each numbered section. Be sure to include and <u>underline</u> all of the vocabulary words in this outline.

1._____   4._____
2._____   5._____
3._____   6._____

IV. Cut along the dotted line to remove the original fable. Rewrite this fable using your outline. Include and <u>underline</u> the vocabulary words in your rewrite. Check your work for the following: neat and graceful handwriting, title, indentation, spelling, punctuation.

The Gnat and the Bull

[1]A gnat settled on the horn of a bull, [2]and sat there a long time. [3]Just as he was about to fly off, he made a buzzing noise, [4]and inquired of the bull if he would like him to go. [5]The bull replied, "I did not know you had come, [6]and I shall not miss you when you go away."

[7]*Some men are of more consequence in their own eyes than in the eyes of their neighbors.*

The Gnat and the Bull   Name:_____

I. List the characters in this fable:_____

II. Vocabulary: <u>Underline</u> the vocabulary words in the fable, and define them below.

1. gnat:_____   3. replied:_____
2. inquired:_____   4. consequence:_____

III. Outline this fable using a three or four word sentence or phrase for each numbered section. Be sure to include and <u>underline</u> all of the vocabulary words in this outline.

1._____   5._____
2._____   6._____
3._____   7._____
4._____

IV. Cut along the dotted line to remove the original fable. Rewrite this fable using your outline. Include and <u>underline</u> the vocabulary words in your rewrite. Check your work for the following: neat and graceful handwriting, title, indentation, spelling, punctuation.

The Fox and the Woodcutter

¹A fox, running before the hounds, came across a woodcutter felling an oak and begged him to show him a safe hiding-place. ²The woodcutter advised him to take shelter in his own hut, so the fox crept in and hid himself in a corner. ³The huntsman soon came up with his hounds and inquired of the woodcutter if he had seen the fox. ⁴He declared that he had not seen him, and yet pointed, all the time he was speaking, to the hut where the fox lay hidden. ⁵The huntsman took no notice of the signs, but believing his word, hastened forward in the chase. ⁶As soon as they were well away, the fox departed without taking any notice of the woodcutter. ⁷Whereon he called to him and reproached him, saying, "⁸You ungrateful fellow, you owe your life to me, and yet you leave me without a word of thanks." ⁹The fox replied, "Indeed, I should have thanked you fervently if your deeds had been as good as your words, and if your hands had not been traitors to your speech."

✂--

The Fox and the Woodcutter   Name:_____

I. List the characters in this fable:_____

II. Vocabulary: <u>Underline</u> the vocabulary words in the fable, and define them below.

1. felling:_____   3. reproached:_____
2. inquired:_____   4. traitors:_____

III. Outline this fable using a three or four word sentence or phrase for each numbered section. Be sure to include and <u>underline</u> all of the vocabulary words in this outline.

1._____   6._____
2._____   7._____
3._____   8._____
4._____   9._____
5._____

IV. Cut along the dotted line to remove the original fable. Rewrite this fable using your outline. Include and <u>underline</u> the vocabulary words in your rewrite. Check your work for the following: neat and graceful handwriting, title, indentation, spelling, punctuation.

The Hare and the Tortoise

¹A hare one day ridiculed the short feet and slow pace of the tortoise, who replied, laughing: ²"Though you be swift as the wind, I will beat you in a race." ³The hare, believing her assertion to be simply impossible, assented to the proposal; ⁴and they agreed that the fox should choose the course and fix the goal. ⁵On the day appointed for the race the two started together. ⁶The tortoise never for a moment stopped, but went on with a slow but steady pace straight to the end of the course. ⁷The hare, trusting to his native swiftness, cared little about the race, and lying down by the wayside, fell fast asleep. ⁸At last waking up, and moving as fast as he could, he saw the tortoise had reached the goal, and was comfortably dozing after her fatigue.

⁹*Slow but steady wins the race.*

The Hare and the Tortoise   Name:_____

I. List the characters in this fable:_____

II. Vocabulary: Underline the vocabulary words in the fable, and define them below.

1. ridiculed:_____ 3. proposal:_____

2. assented:_____ 4. native:_____

III. Outline this fable using a three or four word sentence or phrase for each numbered section. Be sure to include and underline all of the vocabulary words in this outline.

1._____ 6._____

2._____ 7._____

3._____ 8._____

4._____ 9._____

5._____

IV. Cut along the dotted line to remove the original fable. Rewrite this fable using your outline. Include and underline the vocabulary words in your rewrite. Check your work for the following: neat and graceful handwriting, title, indentation, spelling, punctuation.

The Father and His Sons

[1]A father had a family of sons who were perpetually quarreling among themselves. [2]When he failed to heal their disputes by his exhortations, [3]he determined to give them a practical illustration of the evils of disunion; [4]and for this purpose he one day told them to bring him a bundle of sticks. [5]When they had done so, he placed the faggot into the hands of each of them in succession, and ordered them to break it in pieces. [6]They tried with all their strength, and were not able to do it. [7]He next opened the faggot, took the sticks separately, one by one, and again put them into his sons' hands, upon which they broke them easily. [8]He then addressed them in these words: "My sons, if you are of one mind, and unite to assist each other, you will be as this faggot, uninjured by all the attempts of your enemies; [9]but if you are divided among yourselves, you will be broken as easily as these sticks."

The Father and His Sons   Name:_____

I. List the characters in this fable:_____

II. Vocabulary: <u>Underline</u> the vocabulary words in the fable, and define them below.

1. perpetually:_____   3. disunion:_____
2. disputes:_____   4. addressed:_____

III. Outline this fable using a three or four word sentence or phrase for each numbered section. Be sure to include and <u>underline</u> all of the vocabulary words in this outline.

1._____   6._____
2._____   7._____
3._____   8._____
4._____   9._____
5._____

IV. Cut along the dotted line to remove the original fable. Rewrite this fable using your outline. Include and <u>underline</u> the vocabulary words in your rewrite. Check your work for the following: neat and graceful handwriting, title, indentation, spelling, punctuation.

The Wolf and the Lamb

¹A wolf, meeting with a lamb astray from the fold, resolved not to lay violent hands on him, ²but to find some plea to justify to the lamb the wolf's right to eat him. ³He thus addressed him: "Sir, last year you grossly insulted me." ⁴"Indeed," bleated the lamb in a mournful voice, "I was not then born." ⁵Then said the wolf, "You feed in my pasture." ⁶"No, good sir," replied the lamb, "I have not yet tasted grass." ⁷Again said the wolf, "You drink of my well." ⁸"No, exclaimed the lamb, "I never yet drank water, for as yet my mother's milk is both food and drink to me." ⁹Upon which the wolf seized him and ate him up, saying, "Well! I won't remain supperless, even though you refute every one of my imputations."

¹⁰*The tyrant will always find a pretext for his tyranny.*

✂--

The Wolf and the Lamb   Name:_____

I. List the characters in this fable:_____

II. Vocabulary: Underline the vocabulary words in the fable, and define them below.

1. resolved:_____   3. tyrant:_____

2. grossly:_____   4. pretext:_____

III. Outline this fable using a three or four word sentence or phrase for each numbered section. Be sure to include and underline all of the vocabulary words in this outline.

1._____   6._____
2._____   7._____
3._____   8._____
4._____   9._____
5._____   10._____

IV. Cut along the dotted line to remove the original fable. Rewrite this fable using your outline. Include and underline the vocabulary words in your rewrite. Check your work for the following: neat and graceful handwriting, title, indentation, spelling, punctuation.

The Bat and the Weasels

[1]A bat who fell upon the ground and was caught by a weasel pleaded to be spared his life. [2]The weasel refused, saying that he was by nature the enemy of all birds. [3]The bat assured him that he was not a bird, but a mouse, and thus was set free. [4]Shortly afterwards the bat again fell to the ground and was caught by another weasel, whom he likewise entreated not to eat him. [5]The weasel said that he had a special hostility to mice. [6]The bat assured him that he was not a mouse, but a bat, and thus a second time escaped.

[7]*It is wise to turn circumstances to good account.*

✂--

The Bat and the Weasels   Name:_____

I. List the characters in this fable:_____

II. Vocabulary: Underline the vocabulary words in the fable, and define them below.

1. pleaded:_____   3. hostility:_____

2. nature:_____   4. circumstances:_____

III. Outline this fable using a three or four word sentence or phrase for each numbered section. Be sure to include and underline all of the vocabulary words in this outline.

1._____   5._____
2._____   6._____
3._____   7._____
4._____

IV. Cut along the dotted line to remove the original fable. Rewrite this fable using your outline. Include and underline the vocabulary words in your rewrite. Check your work for the following: neat and graceful handwriting, title, indentation, spelling, punctuation.

The Lion and the Mouse

¹A lion was awakened from sleep by a mouse running over his face. ²Rising up angrily, he caught him and was about to kill him, when the mouse piteously entreated, saying: ³"If you would only spare my life, I would be sure to repay you kindness." ⁴The lion laughed and let him go. ⁵It happened shortly after this that the lion was caught by some hunters, who bound him by strong ropes to the ground. ⁶The mouse, recognizing his roar, came up, gnawed the rope with his teeth, and set him free, exclaiming: ⁷"You ridiculed the idea of my ever being able to help you, not expecting to receive from me any repayment of your favor; ⁸but now you know that it is possible for even a mouse to confer benefits on a lion."

✂---

The Lion and the Mouse   Name:_____

I. List the characters in this fable:_____

II. Vocabulary: Underline the vocabulary words in the fable, and define them below.

1. entreated:_____   3. ridiculed:_____

2. spare:_____   4. confer:_____

III. Outline this fable using a three or four word sentence or phrase for each numbered section. Be sure to include and underline all of the vocabulary words in this outline.

1._____   5._____
2._____   6._____
3._____   7._____
4._____   8._____

IV. Cut along the dotted line to remove the original fable. Rewrite this fable using your outline. Include and underline the vocabulary words in your rewrite. Check your work for the following: neat and graceful handwriting, title, indentation, spelling, punctuation.

The Tortoise and the Eagle

¹A tortoise, lazily basking in the sun, complained to the sea-birds of her hard fate, ²that no one would teach her to fly. ³An eagle, hovering near, heard her lamentation and demanded what reward she would give to him if he would take her aloft and float her in the air. ⁴"I will give to you," she said, "all the riches of the Red Sea." ⁵"I will teach you to fly then," said the eagle; ⁶and taking her up in his talons he carried her almost to the clouds-when suddenly he let her go, ⁷and she fell on a lofty mountain, dashing her shell to pieces. ⁸The tortoise exclaimed in the moment of death: ⁹"I have deserved my present fate; ¹⁰for what had I to do with wings and clouds, who can with difficulty move about on the earth?"

¹¹If men had all they wished, they would be often ruined.

The Tortoise and the Eagle   Name:_____

I. List the characters in this fable:_____

II. Vocabulary: <u>Underline</u> the vocabulary words in the fable, and define them below.

1. fate:_____   3. talons:_____
2. lamentation:_____   4. lofty:_____

III. Outline this fable using a three or four word sentence or phrase for each numbered section. Be sure to include and <u>underline</u> all of the vocabulary words in this outline.

1._____   7._____
2._____   8._____
3._____   9._____
4._____   10._____
5._____   11._____
6._____

IV. Cut along the dotted line to remove the original fable. Rewrite this fable using your outline. Include and <u>underline</u> the vocabulary words in your rewrite. Check your work for the following: neat and graceful handwriting, title, indentation, spelling, punctuation.

The Bear and the Two Travelers

¹Two men were traveling together, when a bear suddenly met them on their path. ²One of them climbed up quickly into a tree and concealed himself in the branches. ³The other, seeing that he must be attacked, fell flat on the ground, and when the bear came up and felt him with his snout, and smelt him all over, ⁴he held his breath, and feigned the appearance of death as much as he could. ⁵The bear soon left him, for it is said he will not touch a dead body. ⁶When he was quite gone, the other traveler descended from the tree, ⁷and jocularly inquired of his friend what it was the bear had whispered in his ear. ⁸"He gave me this advice," his companion replied. ⁹"Never travel with a friend who deserts you at the approach of danger."

¹⁰*Misfortune tests the sincerity of friends.*

The Bear and the Two Travelers   Name:_____

I. List the characters in this fable:_____

II. Vocabulary: Underline the vocabulary words in the fable, and define them below.

1. concealed:_____   3. jocularly:_____
2. feigned:_____   4. sincerity:_____

III. Outline this fable using a three or four word sentence or phrase for each numbered section. Be sure to include and underline all of the vocabulary words in this outline.

1._____   6._____
2._____   7._____
3._____   8._____
4._____   9._____
5._____   10._____

IV. Cut along the dotted line to remove the original fable. Rewrite this fable using your outline. Include and underline the vocabulary words in your rewrite. Check your work for the following: neat and graceful handwriting, title, indentation, spelling, punctuation.

The Sick Lion

¹A lion, unable from old age and infirmities to provide himself with food by force, ²resolved to do so by artifice. ³He returned to his den, and lying down there, pretended to be sick, taking care that his sickness should be publicly known. ⁴The beasts expressed their sorrow, and came one by one to his den, where the lion devoured them. ⁵After many of the beasts had thus disappeared, the fox discovered the trick, ⁶and presenting himself to the lion, stood on the outside of the cave, at a respectful distance, and asked him how he was. ⁷"I am very middling," replied the lion, ⁸"but why do you stand without? ⁹Pray enter within to talk with me." ¹⁰"No, thank you," said the fox. ¹¹"I notice that there are many prints of feet entering your cave, but I see no trace of any returning."

¹²*He is wise who is warned by the misfortune of others.*

The Sick Lion   Name:_____

I. List the characters in this fable:_____

II. Vocabulary: <u>Underline</u> the vocabulary words in the fable, and define them below.

1. infirmities:_____   3. pray:_____
2. resolved:_____   4. misfortune:_____

III. Outline this fable using a three or four word sentence or phrase for each numbered section. Be sure to include and <u>underline</u> all of the vocabulary words in this outline.

1._____   7._____
2._____   8._____
3._____   9._____
4._____   10._____
5._____   11._____
6._____   12._____

IV. Cut along the dotted line to remove the original fable. Rewrite this fable using your outline. Include and <u>underline</u> the vocabulary words in your rewrite. Check your work for the following: neat and graceful handwriting, title, indentation, spelling, punctuation.

The Boasting Traveler

[1]A man who had traveled in foreign lands boasted very much on returning to his own country, [2]of the many wonderful and heroic feats he had performed in the different places he had visited. [3]Among other things, he said that when he was at Rhodes he had leaped to such a distance that no man of his day could leap anywhere near him-- [4]and as to that, there were in Rhodes many persons who saw him do it and whom he could call as witnesses. [5]One of the bystanders interrupted him, saying: [6]"Now, my good man, if this be all true there is no need of witnesses. [7]Suppose this to be Rhodes, and leap for us."

The Boasting Traveler   Name:_____

I. List the characters in this fable:_____

II. Vocabulary: <u>Underline</u> the vocabulary words in the fable, and define them below.

1. boasted:_____   3. bystanders:_____

2. witnesses:_____   4. suppose:_____

III. Outline this fable using a three or four word sentence or phrase for each numbered section. Be sure to include and <u>underline</u> all of the vocabulary words in this outline.

1._____   5._____
2._____   6._____
3._____   7._____
4._____

IV. Cut along the dotted line to remove the original fable. Rewrite this fable using your outline. Include and <u>underline</u> the vocabulary words in your rewrite. Check your work for the following: neat and graceful handwriting, title, indentation, spelling, punctuation.

The Oxen and the Butchers

¹The oxen once upon a time sought to destroy the butchers, ²who practiced a trade destructive to their race. ³They assembled on a certain day to carry out their purpose, and sharpened their horns for the contest. ⁴But one of them who was exceedingly old (for many a field had he plowed) thus spoke: ⁵"These butchers, it is true, slaughter us, but they do so with skillful hands, and with no unnecessary pain. ⁶If we get rid of them, we shall fall into the hands of unskillful operators, and thus suffer a double death: ⁶for you may be assured, that though all the butchers should perish, ⁷yet will men ever want beef."

⁸*Do not be in a hurry to change one evil for another.*

The Oxen and the Butchers   Name:_____

I. List the characters in this fable:_____

II. Vocabulary: <u>Underline</u> the vocabulary words in the fable, and define them below.

1. oxen:_____   3. assembled:_____
2. trade:_____   4. exceedingly:_____

III. Outline this fable using a three or four word sentence or phrase for each numbered section. Be sure to include and <u>underline</u> all of the vocabulary words in this outline.

1._____   5._____
2._____   6._____
3._____   7._____
4._____   8._____

IV. Cut along the dotted line to remove the original fable. Rewrite this fable using your outline. Include and <u>underline</u> the vocabulary words in your rewrite. Check your work for the following: neat and graceful handwriting, title, indentation, spelling, punctuation.

The Goatherd and the Wild Goats

¹A goatherd, driving his flock from their pasture at eventide, found some wild goats mingled among them, and shut them up together with his own for the night. ²The next day it snowed very hard, so that he could not take the herd to their usual feeding places, but was obliged to keep them in the fold. ³He gave his own goats just sufficient food to keep them alive, ⁴but fed the strangers more abundantly in the hope of enticing them to stay with him and of making them his own. ⁵When the thaw set in, he led them all out to feed, and the wild goats scampered away as fast as they could to the mountains. ⁶The goatherd scolded them for their ingratitude in leaving him, when during the storm he had taken more care of them than of his own herd. ⁷One of them, turning about, said to him: "That is the very reason why we are so cautious; for if you yesterday treated us better than the goats you have had so long, ⁸it is plain also that if others came after us, you would in the same manner prefer them to ourselves."

⁹Old friends cannot with impunity be sacrificed for new ones.

The Goatherd and the Wild Goats   Name:_____

I. List the characters in this fable:_____

II. Vocabulary: Underline the vocabulary words in the fable, and define them below.

1. eventide:_____   3. ingratitude:_____

2. obliged:_____   4. impunity:_____

III. Outline this fable using a three or four word sentence or phrase for each numbered section. Be sure to include and underline all of the vocabulary words in this outline.

1._____   6._____
2._____   7._____
3._____   8._____
4._____   9._____
5._____

IV. Cut along the dotted line to remove the original fable. Rewrite this fable using your outline. Include and underline the vocabulary words in your rewrite. Check your work for the following: neat and graceful handwriting, title, indentation, spelling, punctuation.

The Fox Who Had Lost His Tail

¹A fox caught in a trap escaped, but in so doing lost his tail. ²Thereafter, feeling his life a burden from the shame and ridicule to which he was exposed, ³he schemed to convince all the other foxes that being tailless was much more attractive, ⁴thus making up for his own deprivation. ⁵He assembled a good many foxes and publicly advised them to cut off their tails, saying that they would not only look much better without them, ⁶but that they would get rid of the weight of the brush, which was a very great inconvenience. ⁷One of them interrupting him said, ⁸"If you had not yourself lost your tail, my friend, you would not thus counsel us."

✂---

The Fox Who Had Lost His Tail   · Name:_____

I. List the characters in this fable:_____

II. Vocabulary: <u>Underline</u> the vocabulary words in the fable, and define them below.

1. ridicule:_____   3. assembled:_____
2. deprivation:_____   4. counsel:_____

III. Outline this fable using a three or four word sentence or phrase for each numbered section. Be sure to include and <u>underline</u> all of the vocabulary words in this outline.

1._____   5._____
2._____   6._____
3._____   7._____
4._____   8._____

IV. Cut along the dotted line to remove the original fable. Rewrite this fable using your outline. Include and <u>underline</u> the vocabulary words in your rewrite. Check your work for the following: neat and graceful handwriting, title, indentation, spelling, punctuation.

The Shepherd's Boy and the Wolf

[1]A shepherd-boy, who watched a flock of sheep near a village, brought out the villagers three or four times by crying out, "Wolf! Wolf!" [2]and when his neighbors came to help him, laughed at them for their pains. [3]The wolf, however, did truly come at last. [4]The shepherd-boy, now really alarmed, shouted in an agony of terror: [5]"Pray, do come and help me; the wolf is killing the sheep"; [6]but no one paid any heed to his cries, nor rendered any assistance. [7]The wolf, having no cause of fear, at his leisure lacerated or destroyed the whole flock.

[8]There is no believing a liar, even when he speaks the truth.

The Shepherd's Boy and the Wolf   Name:_____

I. List the characters in this fable:_____

II. Vocabulary: <u>Underline</u> the vocabulary words in the fable, and define them below.

1. pains:_____ 3. pray:_____

2. agony:_____ 4. lacerated:_____

III. Outline this fable using a three or four word sentence or phrase for each numbered section. Be sure to include and <u>underline</u> all of the vocabulary words in this outline.

1._____ 5._____
2._____ 6._____
3._____ 7._____
4._____ 8._____

IV. Cut along the dotted line to remove the original fable. Rewrite this fable using your outline. Include and <u>underline</u> the vocabulary words in your rewrite. Check your work for the following: neat and graceful handwriting, title, indentation, spelling, punctuation.

The Lion, the Bear, and the Fox

[1]A lion and a bear seized a kid at the same moment, and fought fiercely for its possession. [2]When they had fearfully lacerated each other and were faint from the long combat, [3]they lay down exhausted with fatigue. [4]A fox, who had gone round them at a distance several times, [5]saw them both stretched on the ground with the kid lying untouched in the middle. [6]He ran in between them, and seizing the kid scampered off as fast as he could. [7]The lion and the bear saw him, but not being able to get up, said, [8]"Woe be to us, that we should have fought and belabored ourselves only to serve the turn of a fox!"

[9]*It sometimes happens that one man has all the toil, and another all the profit.*

✂---

The Lion, the Bear, and the Fox   Name:_____

I. List the characters in this fable:_____

II. Vocabulary: Underline the vocabulary words in the fable, and define them below.

1. seized:_____   3. scampered:_____

2. lacerated:_____   4. belabored:_____

III. Outline this fable using a three or four word sentence or phrase for each numbered section. Be sure to include and underline all of the vocabulary words in this outline.

1._____   6._____
2._____   7._____
3._____   8._____
4._____   9._____
5._____

IV. Cut along the dotted line to remove the original fable. Rewrite this fable using your outline. Include and underline the vocabulary words in your rewrite. Check your work for the following: neat and graceful handwriting, title, indentation, spelling, punctuation.

The Gnat and the Lion

¹A gnat came and said to a lion, ²"I do not in the least fear you, nor are you stronger than I am. ³For in what does your strength consist? ⁴You can scratch with your claws and bite with your teeth-so can a woman in her quarrels. ⁵I repeat that I am altogether more powerful than you; and if you doubt it, let us fight and see who will conquer." ⁶The gnat, having sounded his horn, ⁷fastened himself upon the lion and stung him on the nostrils and the parts of the face devoid of hair. ⁸While trying to crush him, the lion tore himself with his claws, until he punished himself severely. ⁹The gnat thus prevailed over the lion, and, buzzing about in a song of triumph, flew away. ¹⁰But shortly afterwards he became entangled in the meshes of a cobweb and was eaten by a spider. ¹¹He greatly lamented his fate, saying, ¹²"Woe is me, that I, who can wage war successfully with the hugest beasts, ¹³should perish myself from this spider, the most inconsiderable of insects!"

The Gnat and the Lion   Name:_____

I. List the characters in this fable:_____

II. Vocabulary: Underline the vocabulary words in the fable, and define them below.

1. quarrels:_____   3. devoid:_____

2. conquer:_____   4. inconsiderable:_____

III. Outline this fable using a three or four word sentence or phrase for each numbered section. Be sure to include and underline all of the vocabulary words in this outline.

1._____   8._____
2._____   9._____
3._____   10._____
4._____   11._____
5._____   12._____
6._____   13._____
7._____

IV. Cut along the dotted line to remove the original fable. Rewrite this fable using your outline. Include and underline the vocabulary words in your rewrite. Check your work for the following: neat and graceful handwriting, title, indentation, spelling, punctuation.

The Peasant and the Eagle

[1]A peasant found an eagle captured in a trap, and much admiring the bird, set him free. [2]The eagle did not prove ungrateful to his deliverer, [3]for seeing the peasant sitting under a wall which was not safe, [4]he flew toward him and with his talons snatched a bundle from his head. [5]When the peasant rose in pursuit, the eagle let the bundle fall again. [6]Taking it up, the man returned to the same place, to find the wall under which he had been sitting had fallen to pieces; [7]and he marveled at the service rendered him by the eagle.

The Peasant and the Eagle   Name:_____

I. List the characters in this fable:_____

II. Vocabulary: Underline the vocabulary words in the fable, and define them below.

1. peasant:_____   3. marveled:_____
2. talons:_____   4. rendered:_____

III. Outline this fable using a three or four word sentence or phrase for each numbered section. Be sure to include and underline all of the vocabulary words in this outline.

1._____   5._____
2._____   6._____
3._____   7._____
4._____

IV. Cut along the dotted line to remove the original fable. Rewrite this fable using your outline. Include and underline the vocabulary words in your rewrite. Check your work for the following: neat and graceful handwriting, title, indentation, spelling, punctuation.

The Ant and the Dove

¹An ant went to the bank of a river to quench its thirst, ²and being carried away by the rush of the stream, was on the point of drowning. ³A dove sitting on a tree overhanging the water plucked a leaf and let it fall into the stream close to her. ⁴The ant climbed onto it and floated in safety to the bank. ⁵Shortly afterwards a bird catcher came and stood under the tree, and laid his lime-twigs for the dove, which sat in the branches. ⁶The ant, perceiving his design, stung him in the foot. ⁷In pain the bird catcher threw down the twigs, and the noise made the dove take wing.

✂--

The Ant and the Dove   Name:_____

I. List the characters in this fable:_____

II. Vocabulary: <u>Underline</u> the vocabulary words in the fable, and define them below.

1. quench:_____ 3. design:_____
2. perceiving:_____ 4. take wing:_____

III. Outline this fable using a three or four word sentence or phrase for each numbered section. Be sure to include and <u>underline</u> all of the vocabulary words in this outline.

1._____ 5._____
2._____ 6._____
3._____ 7._____
4._____

IV. Cut along the dotted line to remove the original fable. Rewrite this fable using your outline. Include and <u>underline</u> the vocabulary words in your rewrite. Check your work for the following: neat and graceful handwriting, title, indentation, spelling, punctuation.

The Two Frogs

¹Two frogs were neighbors. ²One inhabited a deep pond, far removed from public view; ³the other lived in a gully containing little water, and traversed by a country road. ⁴The frog that lived in the pond warned his friend to change his residence and entreated him to come and live with him, ⁵saying that he would enjoy greater safety from danger and more abundant food. ⁶The other refused, saying that he felt it so very hard to leave a place to which he had become accustomed. ⁷A few days afterwards a heavy wagon passed through the gully and crushed him to death under its wheels.

⁸*A willful man will have his way to his own hurt.*

The Two Frogs   Name:_____

I. List the characters in this fable:_____

II. Vocabulary: <u>Underline</u> the vocabulary words in the fable, and define them below.

1. inhabited:_____   3. residence:_____

2. gully:_____   4. abundant:_____

III. Outline this fable using a three or four word sentence or phrase for each numbered section. Be sure to include and <u>underline</u> all of the vocabulary words in this outline.

1._____   5._____
2._____   6._____
3._____   7._____
4._____   8._____

IV. Cut along the dotted line to remove the original fable. Rewrite this fable using your outline. Include and <u>underline</u> the vocabulary words in your rewrite. Check your work for the following: neat and graceful handwriting, title, indentation, spelling, punctuation.

The Jackdaw and the Doves

¹A jackdaw, seeing some doves in a cote abundantly provided with food, ²painted himself white and joined them in order to share their plentiful maintenance. ³The doves, as long as he was silent, supposed him to be one of themselves and admitted him to their cote. ⁴But when one day he forgot himself and began to chatter, ⁵they discovered his true character and drove him forth, pecking him with their beaks. ⁶Failing to obtain food among the doves, he returned to the jackdaws. ⁷They too, not recognizing him on account of his color, ⁸expelled him from living with them. ⁹So desiring two ends, he obtained neither.

✂--

The Jackdaw and the Doves   Name:_____

I. List the characters in this fable:_____

II. Vocabulary: Underline the vocabulary words in the fable, and define them below.

1. cote:_____   3. obtain:_____
2. maintenance:_____   4. expelled:_____

III. Outline this fable using a three or four word sentence or phrase for each numbered section. Be sure to include and underline all of the vocabulary words in this outline.

1._____   6._____
2._____   7._____
3._____   8._____
4._____   9._____
5._____

IV. Cut along the dotted line to remove the original fable. Rewrite this fable using your outline. Include and underline the vocabulary words in your rewrite. Check your work for the following: neat and graceful handwriting, title, indentation, spelling, punctuation.

The Wolf and the Shepherd

¹A wolf followed a flock of sheep for a long time and did not attempt to injure one of them. ²The shepherd at first stood on his guard against him, ³as against an enemy, and kept a strict watch over his movements. ⁴But when the wolf, day after day, kept in the company of the sheep and did not make the slightest effort to seize them, ⁵the shepherd began to look upon him as a guardian of his flock rather than as a plotter of evil against it; ⁶and when the occasion called him one day to the city, ⁷he left the sheep entirely in his charge. ⁸The wolf, now that he had the opportunity, ⁹fell upon the sheep, and destroyed the greater part of the flock. ¹⁰When the shepherd returned to find his flock destroyed, he exclaimed: ¹¹"I have been rightly served; why did I trust my sheep to a wolf?"

✂ ---

The Wolf and the Shepherd   Name:_____

I. List the characters in this fable:_____

II. Vocabulary: <u>Underline</u> the vocabulary words in the fable, and define them below.

1. seize:_____   3. occasion:_____

2. guardian:_____   4. exclaimed:_____

III. Outline this fable using a three or four word sentence or phrase for each numbered section. Be sure to include and <u>underline</u> all of the vocabulary words in this outline.

1._____   7._____
2._____   8._____
3._____   9._____
4._____   10._____
5._____   11._____
6._____

IV. Cut along the dotted line to remove the original fable. Rewrite this fable using your outline. Include and <u>underline</u> the vocabulary words in your rewrite. Check your work for the following: neat and graceful handwriting, title, indentation, spelling, punctuation.

The Lion and the Bull

¹A lion, greatly desiring to capture a bull, and yet afraid to attack him on account of his great size, ²resorted to a trick to ensure his destruction. ³He approached the bull and said, ⁴"I have slain a fine sheep, my friend; and if you will come home and partake of them with me, ⁵I shall be delighted to have your company." ⁶The lion said this in the hope that, as the bull was in the act of reclining to eat, he might attack him, and make his meal on him. ⁷The bull, on approaching the lion's den, saw the huge spits and giant caldrons, ⁸and no sign whatever of the sheep, and, without saying a word, quietly took his departure. ⁹The lion inquired why he went off so abruptly without a word of salutation to his host, ¹⁰who had not given him any cause for offense. ¹¹"I have reasons enough," said the bull. ¹²"I see no indication whatever of your having slaughtered a sheep, ¹³while I do see very plainly every preparation for your dining on a bull."

The Lion and the Bull   Name:_____

I. List the characters in this fable:_____

II. Vocabulary: Underline the vocabulary words in the fable, and define them below.

1. partake:_____   3. salutation:_____
2. caldrons:_____   4. indication:_____

III. Outline this fable using a three or four word sentence or phrase for each numbered section. Be sure to include and underline all of the vocabulary words in this outline.

1._____   8._____
2._____   9._____
3._____   10._____
4._____   11._____
5._____   12._____
6._____   13._____
7._____

IV. Cut along the dotted line to remove the original fable. Rewrite this fable using your outline. Include and underline the vocabulary words in your rewrite. Check your work for the following: neat and graceful handwriting, title, indentation, spelling, punctuation.

The Fowler and the Viper

¹A fowler, taking his bird-lime and his twigs, ²went out to catch birds. ³Seeing a thrush sitting upon a tree, he wished to take it, ⁴and fitting his twigs to a proper length, watched intently, having his whole thoughts directed towards the sky. ⁵While thus looking upwards, he unknowingly trod upon a viper asleep just before his feet. ⁶The viper, turning about, stung him, and falling into a swoon, the man said to himself, ⁷"Woe is me! ⁸That while I purposed to hunt another, ⁹I am myself fallen unawares into the snares of death."

✂--

The Fowler and the Viper   Name:_____

I. List the characters in this fable:_____

II. Vocabulary: <u>Underline</u> the vocabulary words in the fable, and define them below.

1. fowler:_____   3. trod:_____
2. thrush:_____   4. viper:_____

III. Outline this fable using a three or four word sentence or phrase for each numbered section. Be sure to include and <u>underline</u> all of the vocabulary words in this outline.

1._____   6._____
2._____   7._____
3._____   8._____
4._____   9._____
5._____

IV. Cut along the dotted line to remove the original fable. Rewrite this fable using your outline. Include and <u>underline</u> the vocabulary words in your rewrite. Check your work for the following: neat and graceful handwriting, title, indentation, spelling, punctuation.

The North Wind and the Sun

[1]The north wind and the sun disputed as to which was the most powerful, [2]and agreed that he should be declared the victor who could first strip a wayfaring man of his clothes. [3]The north wind first tried his power and blew with all his might, [4]but the keener his blasts, the closer the traveler wrapped his cloak around him, [5]until at last, resigning all hope of victory, the wind called upon the sun to see what he could do. [6]The sun suddenly shone out with all his warmth. [7]The traveler no sooner felt his genial rays than he took off one garment after another, and at last, [8]fairly overcome with heat, [9]undressed and bathed in a stream that lay in his path.

[10]Persuasion is better than force.

The North Wind and the Sun   Name:_____

I. List the characters in this fable:_____

II. Vocabulary: Underline the vocabulary words in the fable, and define them below.

1. disputed:_____   3. resigning:_____

2. keener:_____   4. genial:_____

III. Outline this fable using a three or four word sentence or phrase for each numbered section. Be sure to include and underline all of the vocabulary words in this outline.

1._____	6._____
2._____	7._____
3._____	8._____
4._____	9._____
5._____	10._____

IV. Cut along the dotted line to remove the original fable. Rewrite this fable using your outline. Include and underline the vocabulary words in your rewrite. Check your work for the following: neat and graceful handwriting, title, indentation, spelling, punctuation.

The Sparrow and the Hare

¹A hare, pounced upon by an eagle, sobbed very much and uttered cries like a child. ²A sparrow upbraided her and said, ³"Where now is thy remarkable swiftness of foot? ⁴Why are your feet so slow?" ⁵While the sparrow was thus speaking, a hawk suddenly seized him and killed him. ⁶The hare was comforted in her death, and expiring said, ⁷"Ah! you who so lately, when you supposed yourself safe, exulted over my calamity, ⁸have now reason to deplore a similar misfortune."

The Sparrow and the Hare   Name:_____

I. List the characters in this fable:_____

II. Vocabulary: <u>Underline</u> the vocabulary words in the fable, and define them below.

1. sobbed:_____   3. expiring:_____
2. upbraided:_____   4. calamity:_____

III. Outline this fable using a three or four word sentence or phrase for each numbered section. Be sure to include and <u>underline</u> all of the vocabulary words in this outline.

1._____   5._____
2._____   6._____
3._____   7._____
4._____   8._____

IV. Cut along the dotted line to remove the original fable. Rewrite this fable using your outline. Include and <u>underline</u> the vocabulary words in your rewrite. Check your work for the following: neat and graceful handwriting, title, indentation, spelling, punctuation.

The Eagle and the Jackdaw

¹An eagle, flying down from his perch on a lofty rock, ²seized upon a lamb and carried him aloft in his talons. ³A jackdaw, who witnessed the capture of the lamb, ⁴was stirred with envy and determined to emulate the strength and flight of the eagle. ⁵He flew around with a great whirr of his wings and settled upon a large ram, ⁶with the intention of carrying him off, ⁷but his claws became entangled in the ram's fleece and he was not able to release himself, although he fluttered with his feathers as much as he could. ⁸The shepherd, seeing what had happened, ran up an caught him. ⁹He at once clipped the jackdaw's wings, and taking him home at night, gave him to his children. ¹⁰On their saying, "Father, what kind of bird is it?" he replied, ¹¹"To my certain knowledge he is a daw; but he would like you to think an eagle."

The Eagle and the Jackdaw   Name:_____

I. List the characters in this fable:_____

II. Vocabulary: <u>Underline</u> the vocabulary words in the fable, and define them below.

1. lofty:_____   3. emulate:_____
2. jackdaw:_____   4. entangled:_____

III. Outline this fable using a three or four word sentence or phrase for each numbered section. Be sure to include and <u>underline</u> all of the vocabulary words in this outline.

1._____   7._____
2._____   8._____
3._____   9._____
4._____   10._____
5._____   11._____
6._____

IV. Cut along the dotted line to remove the original fable. Rewrite this fable using your outline. Include and <u>underline</u> the vocabulary words in your rewrite. Check your work for the following: neat and graceful handwriting, title, indentation, spelling, punctuation.

The Stag at the Pool

[1]A stag overpowered by heat came to a spring to drink. [2]Seeing his own shadow reflected in the water, he greatly admired the size and variety of his horns, [3]but felt angry with himself for having such slender and weak feet. [4]While he was thus contemplating himself, a lion appeared at the pool and crouched to spring upon him. [5]The stag immediately took to flight, and exerting his utmost speed, [6]as long as the plain was smooth and open kept himself easily at a safe distance from the lion. [7]But entering a wood he became entangled by his horns, [8]and the lion quickly came up to him and caught him. [9]When too late, he thus reproached himself: [10]"Woe is me! How I have deceived myself! [11]These feet which would have saved me I despised, [12]and I gloried in these antlers which have proved my destruction."

[13]*What is most truly valuable is often underrated.*

The Stag at the Pool   Name:_____

I. List the characters in this fable:_____

II. Vocabulary: Underline the vocabulary words in the fable, and define them below.

1. admired:_____   3. despised:_____
2. contemplating:_____   4. underrated:_____

III. Outline this fable using a three or four word sentence or phrase for each numbered section. Be sure to include and underline all of the vocabulary words in this outline.

1._____   8._____
2._____   9._____
3._____   10._____
4._____   11._____
5._____   12._____
6._____   13._____
7._____

IV. Cut along the dotted line to remove the original fable. Rewrite this fable using your outline. Include and underline the vocabulary words in your rewrite. Check your work for the following: neat and graceful handwriting, title, indentation, spelling, punctuation.

The Two Soldiers and the Robber

¹Two soldiers traveling together were set upon by a robber. ²The one fled away; the other stood his ground and defended himself with his stout right hand. ³The robber being slain, the timid companion ran up and drew his sword, and then, ⁴throwing back his traveling cloak, said, "I'll at him, and I'll take care he shall learn whom he has attacked." ⁵On this, he who had fought with the robber made answer, ⁶"I only wish that you had helped me just now, ⁷even if it had been only with those words, ⁸for I should have been more encouraged, believing them to be true; ⁹but now put up your sword in its sheath and hold your equally useless tongue, ¹⁰till you can deceive others who do not know you. ¹¹I, indeed, who have experienced with what speed you run away, ¹²know right well that no dependence can be placed on your valor."

The Two Soldiers and the Robber   Name:_____

I. List the characters in this fable: _____

II. Vocabulary: <u>Underline</u> the vocabulary words in the fable, and define them below.

1. stout:_____   3. dependence:_____
2. timid:_____   4. valor:_____

III. Outline this fable using a three or four word sentence or phrase for each numbered section. Be sure to include and <u>underline</u> all of the vocabulary words in this outline.

1._____   7._____
2._____   8._____
3._____   9._____
4._____   10._____
5._____   11._____
6._____   12._____

IV. Cut along the dotted line to remove the original fable. Rewrite this fable using your outline. Include and <u>underline</u> the vocabulary words in your rewrite. Check your work for the following: neat and graceful handwriting, title, indentation, spelling, punctuation.

The King's Son and the Painted Lion

¹A king, whose only son was fond of martial exercises, had a dream in which he was warned that his son would be killed by a lion. ²Afraid the dream should prove true, he built for his son a pleasant palace and adorned its walls for his amusement with all kinds of life-sized animals, ³among which was the picture of a lion. ⁴When the young prince saw this, his grief at being thus confined burst out afresh, and, standing near the lion, he said: ⁵"O you most detestable of animals! Through a lying dream of my father's, which he saw in his sleep, I am shut up on your account in this palace as if I had been a girl: what shall I now do to you?" ⁶With these words he stretched out his hands toward a thorn-tree, ⁷meaning to cut a stick from its branches so that he might beat the lion. ⁸But one of the tree's prickles pierced his finger and caused great pain and inflammation, ⁹so that the young prince fell down in a fainting fit. ¹⁰A violent fever suddenly set in, ¹¹from which he died not many days later.

¹²*We had better bear our troubles bravely than try to escape them.*

✂---

The King's Son and the Painted Lion   Name:_____

I. List the characters in this fable:_____

II. Vocabulary: Underline the vocabulary words in the fable, and define them below.

1. adorned:_____   3. inflammation:_____
2. detestable:_____   4. violent:_____

III. Outline this fable using a three or four word sentence or phrase for each numbered section. Be sure to include and underline all of the vocabulary words in this outline.

1._____   7._____
2._____   8._____
3._____   9._____
4._____   10._____
5._____   11._____
6._____   12._____

IV. Cut along the dotted line to remove the original fable. Rewrite this fable using your outline. Include and underline the vocabulary words in your rewrite. Check your work for the following: neat and graceful handwriting, title, indentation, spelling, punctuation.

The Shipwrecked Man and the Sea

¹A shipwrecked man, having been cast upon a certain shore, ²slept after his buffetings with the deep. ³After a while he awoke, and looking upon the sea, ⁴loaded it with reproaches. ⁵He argued that it enticed men with the calmness of its looks, ⁶but when it had induced them to plow its waters, ⁷it grew rough and destroyed them. ⁸The sea, assuming the form of a woman, replied to him: ⁹"Blame not me, my good sir, but the winds, ¹⁰for I am by my own nature as calm and firm even as this earth; ¹¹but the winds suddenly falling on me create these waves, and lash me into fury."

The Shipwrecked Man and the Sea   Name:_____

I. List the characters in this fable:_____

II. Vocabulary: Underline the vocabulary words in the fable, and define them below.

1. reproaches:_____   3. induced:_____

2. enticed:_____   4. fury:_____

III. Outline this fable using a three or four word sentence or phrase for each numbered section. Be sure to include and underline all of the vocabulary words in this outline.

1._____   7._____
2._____   8._____
3._____   9._____
4._____   10._____
5._____   11._____
6._____

IV. Cut along the dotted line to remove the original fable. Rewrite this fable using your outline. Include and underline the vocabulary words in your rewrite. Check your work for the following: neat and graceful handwriting, title, indentation, spelling, punctuation.

The Lion and the Shepherd

[1]A lion, roaming through a forest, trod upon a thorn. [2]Soon afterward he came up to a shepherd and fawned upon him, wagging his tail as if to say, [3]"I am a suppliant, and seek your aid." [4]The shepherd boldly examined the beast, discovered the thorn, and placing his paw upon his lap, pulled it out; [5]thus relieved of his pain, the lion returned into the forest. [6]Some time after, the shepherd, being imprisoned on a false accusation, [7]was condemned "to be cast to the lions" as the punishment for his imputed crime. [8]But when the lion was released from his cage, he recognized the shepherd as the man who healed him, [9]and instead of attacking him, approached and placed his foot upon his lap. [10]The king, as soon as he heard the tale, ordered the lion to be set free again in the forest, [11]and the shepherd to be pardoned and restored to his friends.

✂--

The Lion and the Shepherd   Name:_____

I. List the characters in this fable:_____

II. Vocabulary: Underline the vocabulary words in the fable, and define them below.

1. trod:_____   3. accusation:_____

2. fawned:_____   4. pardoned:_____

III. Outline this fable using a three or four word sentence or phrase for each numbered section. Be sure to include and underline all of the vocabulary words in this outline.

1._____   7._____
2._____   8._____
3._____   9._____
4._____   10._____
5._____   11._____
6._____

IV. Cut along the dotted line to remove the original fable. Rewrite this fable using your outline. Include and underline the vocabulary words in your rewrite. Check your work for the following: neat and graceful handwriting, title, indentation, spelling, punctuation.

The Panther and the Shepherds

¹A panther, by some mischance, fell into a pit. ²The shepherds discovered him, and some threw sticks at him and pelted him with stones, ³while others, moved with compassion towards one about to die even though no one should hurt him, threw in some food to prolong his life. ⁴At night they returned home, not dreaming of any danger, but supposing that on the morrow they would find him dead. ⁵The panther, however, when he had recruited his feeble strength, freed himself with a sudden bound from the pit, ⁶and hastened to his den with rapid steps. ⁷After a few days he came forth and slaughtered the cattle, and, ⁸killing the shepherds who had attacked him, raged with angry fury. ⁹Then they who had spared his life, fearing for their safety, ¹⁰surrendered to him their flocks and begged only for their lives. ¹¹To them the panther made this reply: "I remember alike those who sought my life with stones, and those who gave me food, lay aside, therefore, your fears. ¹²I return as an enemy only to those who injured me."

The Panther and the Shepherds   Name:_____

I. List the characters in this fable:_____

II. Vocabulary: <u>Underline</u> the vocabulary words in the fable, and define them below.

1. mischance:_____   3. recruited:_____

2. morrow:_____   4. spared:_____

III. Outline this fable using a three or four word sentence or phrase for each numbered section. Be sure to include and <u>underline</u> all of the vocabulary words in this outline.

1._____	7._____
2._____	8._____
3._____	9._____
4._____	10._____
5._____	11._____
6._____	12._____

IV. Cut along the dotted line to remove the original fable. Rewrite this fable using your outline. Include and <u>underline</u> the vocabulary words in your rewrite. Check your work for the following: neat and graceful handwriting, title, indentation, spelling, punctuation.

The Kingdom of the Lion

¹The beasts of the field and forest had a lion as their king. ²He was neither wrathful, cruel, nor tyrannical, but just and gentle as a king could be. ³During his reign he made a royal proclamation for the general assembly of all the birds and beasts, ⁴and drew up conditions for a universal league, ⁵in which the wolf and the lamb, the panther and the kid, the tiger and the stag, the dog and the hare, ⁶should live together in perfect peace and amity. ⁷The hare said, "Oh, how I have longed to see this day, ⁸in which the weak shall take their place with impunity by the side of the strong." ⁹And after the hare said this, he ran for his life.

✂--

The Kingdom of the Lion Name:_____

I. List the characters in this fable:_____

II. Vocabulary: <u>Underline</u> the vocabulary words in the fable, and define them below.

1. tyrannical:_____ 3. league:_____
2. proclamation:_____ 4. impunity:_____

III. Outline this fable using a three or four word sentence or phrase for each numbered section. Be sure to include and <u>underline</u> all of the vocabulary words in this outline.

1._____ 6._____
2._____ 7._____
3._____ 8._____
4._____ 9._____
5._____

IV. Cut along the dotted line to remove the original fable. Rewrite this fable using your outline. Include and <u>underline</u> the vocabulary words in your rewrite. Check your work for the following: neat and graceful handwriting, title, indentation, spelling, punctuation.

The Town Mouse and the Country Mouse

[1]A country mouse invited a town mouse, an intimate friend, to pay him a visit and partake of his country fare. [2]As they were on the bare plowlands, eating their wheat-stalks and roots pulled up from the hedgerow, the town mouse said to his friend, [3]"You live here the life of the ants, while in my house is the horn of plenty. I am surrounded with every luxury, and if you will come with me, as I wish you would, you shall have an ample share of my dainties." [4]The country mouse was easily persuaded, and returned to town with his friend. [5]On his arrival, the town mouse placed before him bread, barley, beans, dried figs, honey, raisins, and, last of all, brought a dainty piece of cheese from a basket. [6]The country mouse, being much delighted at the sight of such good cheer, expressed his satisfaction in warm terms and lamented his own hard fate. [7]Just as they were beginning to eat, someone opened the door, and they both ran off squeaking, as fast as they could, to a hole so narrow that two could only find room in it by squeezing. [8]They had scarcely begun their repast again when someone else entered to take something out of the cupboard, [9]whereupon the two mice, more frightened than before, ran away and hid themselves. [10]At last the country mouse, almost famished, said to his friend: "Although you have prepared for me so dainty a feast, I must leave you to enjoy it by yourself. [11]It is surrounded by too many dangers to please me. [12]I prefer my bare plowlands and roots from the hedgerow, where I can live in safety, and without fear."

The Town Mouse and the Country Mouse   Name:_____

I. List the characters in this fable:_____

II. Vocabulary: <u>Underline</u> the vocabulary words in the fable, and define them below.

1. intimate:_____   3. lamented:_____

2. luxury:_____   4. famished:_____

III. Outline this fable using a three or four word sentence or phrase for each numbered section. Be sure to include and <u>underline</u> all of the vocabulary words in this outline.

1._____   7._____
2._____   8._____
3._____   9._____
4._____   10._____
5._____   11._____
6._____   12._____

IV. Cut along the dotted line to remove the original fable. Rewrite this fable using your outline. Include and <u>underline</u> the vocabulary words in your rewrite. Check your work for the following: neat and graceful handwriting, title, indentation, spelling, punctuation.